MAKE ME LAUGH!

THE SKY'S THE LIMIT

NATURALLY FUNNY JOKES

by Rick and Ann Walton with Scott K.
Peterson and Peter and Connie Roop
pictures by Brian Gable

Carolrhoda Books, Inc. • Minneapolis

Q: What kind of coats do trees wear?
A: Douglas firs.

Q: What flowers live in pickle jars?
A: Daffo-dills.

Q: Where should you keep the wind?
A: In an air pocket.

Q: What is a tree's favorite fruit?
A: Pineapple.

Q: What kind of salad do snowmen eat?
A: Cold-slaw.

Q: What do space squirrels like to eat?
A: Astro-nuts.

Q: Why do pine trees buy only ice cream?
A: Because they already have the cones.

Q: What do snowmen put on their faces to keep them looking young?
A: Cold cream.

Q: What do snowmen put on their faces to keep them looking even younger?
A: Ice cream.

Q: What kind of plant likes gymnastics?
A: A tumbleweed.

Q: Why shouldn't you wear snowshoes?
A: Because they'll melt.

Q: What do you get when you cross a barn with a pine tree?

A: A needle in a haystack.

Q: Why did the tree pack her trunk?

A: Because she was leafing town.

Q: If an athlete gets athlete's foot, what does an astronaut get?

A: Missile-toe.

Q: Why are snowmen careful not to get into trouble?

A: Because they don't want to be in hot water.

Q: Why do windows have panes?

A: Because the rain beats on them.

Q: Why was the spruce tree so sad?

A: Because she was a blue spruce.

Q: Why didn't the tree play checkers?

A: Because she was a chess-nut.

Q: What do you get if you're hit by an icicle?

A: A cold sore.

Q: What did the sun say to the snowman?

A: "I thaw you!"

Q: What do well-dressed snowmen wear?
A: Snowsuits.

Q: Why did the sheriff put the star in jail?
A: It was a shooting star.

Q: What kind of flowers can you find in zoos?
A: Tiger lilies.

Q: What flowers talk during April and May?

A: Two lips.

Q: What did one maple tree say to the other?

A: "You sure are a sap."

Q: How do you know when a snowstorm is saying good-bye?

A: You can see a cold wave.

Q: What can you catch if you go ice fishing?

A: A cold.

Q: What should you wear if you want to go out in a hailstorm?

A: A hail-met.

Q: Why did the woman bury all her change in the garden?

A: She wanted to have rich soil for her plants.

Q: What does the sun drink out of?
A: Sunglasses.

Q: What kind of trees do Gypsies read?
A: Palm trees.

Q: What do clouds wear when it gets cold?
A: Raincoats.

Q: What do clouds wear under their raincoats?
A: Thunder-wear.

Q: What are the best days for astronauts to go into space?
A: Moon-day and Saturn-day.

Q: What's the hardest storm to sweep up?
A: A dust storm.

Q: What holds up the moon?
A: Moonbeams.

Q: What kind of dog floats in the air?

A: An Airedale.

Q: What do you get if an Airedale floats too near the sun?

A: A hot dog.

Q: Why did the astronaut take a mop into space?

A: To clean up the stardust.

Q: How do trees clap?

A: With their palms.

Q: What flower has the best eyesight?

A: The iris.

Q: Where should you keep your clouds?

A: In a cloud bank.

Q: Why was the tree wearing sunglasses and carrying a towel?

A: Because he was a beech tree.

Q: What's the weather always like at parades?

A: Partly crowdy.

Q: What goes up when you count down?

A: A rocket.

Q: How did the corn plant lose all her money?

A: By playing the stalk market.

Q: How do you lock a storm door?

A: With a thunderbolt.

Q: Why did the tree want to be a jeweler?

A: Because he had so many rings.

Q: What kind of years weigh the least?

A: Light years.

Q: Where can you buy a storm?

A: From a storm cellar.

Q: What kind of flowers can you find in space?

A: Sunflowers.

Q: Why are trees so successful?

A: Because they are always reaching new heights.

Q: What does the sun eat off of?

A: A hot plate.

Q: How can you tell if it's going to rain cats and dogs?

A: The wind will begin to howl.

Q: What's the temperature like when it rains cats and dogs?

A: It's biting cold.

Q: Why wouldn't the banker give the tree a loan?

A: Because she didn't want to go out on a limb.

Q: Why did the twigs go to Washington?

A: Because they wanted to belong to different branches of the government.

Q: What knocks down houses and makes people laugh?

A: A cy-clown.

Q: Why did the cow jump over the moon?

A: To get to the Milky Way.

Q: Why didn't the maple trust the oak tree?

A: Because the oak looked a little shady.

Q: What did Mr. and Mrs. Tree name their son?

A: Woodrow.

Q: Why are flowers such good friends?

A: Because they started out as buds.

Q: Why did the astronaut take a shovel into space?

A: To dig a black hole.

Q: How do you hold up the sky during the daytime?

A: With sunbeams.

Q: Why do thin cowboys make good astronauts?

A: They're good at sitting in a saddle-light.

Q: Where do trees keep their luggage?

A: In their trunks.

Q: When is the earth cleanest?

A: Right after it showers.

Q: Why should stars wear braces?

A: Because there's so much space between them.

Q: Why are vines so lazy?

A: Because all they want to do is hang around.

Q: What's the best way to keep from getting wet when you go outside?

A: Don't go out when it's raining.

Q: How does an astronaut keep up his pants?

A: With an asteroid belt!

Q: What did one shrub say to the other shrub?

A: "I'm bushed."

Q: What do you get when a cloudburst hits a flock of ducks?

A: A downpour.

Q: Why doesn't Mother Nature cover the grass in water every morning?

A: She doesn't want to over-dew it.

Q: Where do Martians go fishing?

A: In the galax-seas.

Q: Why didn't the satellite go very far?

A: It kept going around in circles.

Q: What happened to the tree who came home late?

A: He was grounded.

Q: What's stranger than when it rains cats and dogs?

A: When kings rain.

Q: What's even stranger than kings raining?

A: Baby showers.

Q: How is a telephone like the planet Saturn?

A: They both have rings.

Q: What tree tires easily?

A: A rubber tree.

Q: Why did the astronaut take an American flag into space?

A: It was a star-spangled banner.

Q: What flower is the king of the garden?

A: The dandy-lion.

Q: Why don't flowers talk?

A: Because it's hard to get them to open up.

Q: Why was the bush always fibbing?

A: Because she was a lie-lac.

Q: What makes a cloudburst?

A: A windbreaker.

Q: What's an astronaut's favorite fish?

A: Starfish.

Q: How does the man in the moon cut his hair?

A: Eclipse-it.

Q: Why is the sun a welcome guest at parties?

A: Because the sun knows how to break the ice.

Q: What's the difference between fog and a falling star?

A: One is mist on earth, and the other is missed in space.

Q: Why are acorns so obnoxious?

A: Because they are always acting like nuts.

Q: Why did the singer go up into space?

A: She wanted to become a star.

Q: Why did the plant go on stage?

A: He wanted to be under the lights.

Q: What do space toads have all over their bodies?

A: Star warts!

Q: Why is the sun so bright?

A: Because it has millions of degrees.

Q: What did the Egyptians call their flowers?

A: Mum-mies.

Q: Why didn't the girl flower go out with the boy flower?

A: Because he never aster.

Q: When do you know that the weather's sad?

A: When you hear the wind wailing.

Q: What do snowmen ride?

A: Ice-cycles.

Q: Where do astronauts go to college?

A: UFO—University for Orbiting.

Q: Why can't you find a comb in a jungle?

A: Because there is so much brush.

Q: What time is it when a Martian peeks in your window?

A: Time to close the blinds!

Q: What do you get when you cross the sun with a goose?

A: Sundown.

Q: Why did the tree take a bath?

A: Because she wanted to spruce herself up.

Q: How can you tell when two vines are in love?

A: Because they are always clinging to each other.

Q: How do trees relax?

A: They get together and shoot the breeze.

Q: What's the best way to shoot the breeze?

A: With an air rifle.

Q: What kind of shots do astronauts get?

A: Boosters.

Q: What does the breeze blow?

A: Wind instruments.

Q: Why do astronauts enjoy space travel?

A: It's out of this world!

Q: Why is thunder so noisy?

A: Because it uses a cloud-speaker.

Q: What are clouds' favorite wind instruments?

A: Foghorns.

Q: What's the best way to talk to a Martian?

A: By long distance!

Q: What did the North Star say to the Big Dipper?

A: "It's not polite to point!"

Q: How do you protect yourself from an angry windstorm.

A: With a windshield.

Q: How do you know when the moon isn't hungry?

A: When it's full!

Q: What kind of music do astronauts like?

A: Nep-tunes.

Q: Why couldn't the trees figure out the riddle?

A: Because they were all stumped.

Q: What's the difference between a thunderstorm and a sore lion?

A: One pours with rain, while the other roars with pain.

Q: Who saves clouds from danger?

A: Thunderdog.

Q: What does the runner-up in the Ms. Galaxy contest receive?

A: A constellation prize.

Q: Why don't some people like trees?

A: Because they think that trees are for the birds.

Q: What do you get when you cross a snowstorm with a cornfield?

A: Cornflakes.

Q: Which astronaut goes into space the most?

A: Sir Launch-a-lot.

Q: Why do snow shovelers make a lot of money?

A: Because there's no business like snow business.

Q: What do you find in a snowbank?

A: Cold cash.

Q: What do you get when you cross an evergreen tree with a pig?

A: A porky-pine.

Q: Why can't a Martian's nose be twelve inches long?

A: If it were, it would be a foot!

Q: Why shouldn't you go up in the sky during a heavy storm?

A: Because it's already overclouded.

Q: Why is there always a kitten by the swamp?

A: Because he's looking for his cattails.

Q: What do you get if you put a mousetrap in your freezer?

A: A cold snap.

Q: Why wouldn't the tree settle down in one spot?

A: Because she was made of driftwood.

Q: What did one tree say to the other?

A: I think it's time we split.

Q: How did the first person ever hit by lightning feel?

A: Shocked.

Q: How do old storms travel fast?

A: They use hurrycanes.

Q: Why did the trees bow?

A: Because the thunder clapped.

Q: How do you capture a fly from outer space?

A: Use a Venus flytrap.

Q: What tree has the most bark?
A: A dogwood.

Q: Who is the king of winter?
A: Old King Cold.

Q: What does Old King Cold do?
A: He rains.

Q: Where does Old King Cold live?
A: Castles in the air.

Q: How can animals tell what the weather's going to be like?
A: They look at the fur-cast.

Q: Where do nice children plant flowers?
A: In a kinder-garden.

Q: What do cats like to do in the winter?
A: Go mice skating.

This book is available in two editions:
Library binding by Carolrhoda Books, Inc.,
  a division of Lerner Publishing Group
Soft cover by First Avenue Editions,
  an imprint of Lerner Publishing Group
241 First Avenue North
Minneapolis, MN 55401 U.S.A.

Website address: www.carolrhodabooks.com

Library of Congress Cataloging-in-Publication Data

    The sky's the limit : naturally funny jokes / by Rick Walton [et al.] ; pictures by
Brian Gable.
        p.   cm. — (Make me laugh!)
    Summary: Presents a variety of jokes about nature.
    ISBN: 1–57505–663–1 (lib. bdg. : alk. paper)
    ISBN: 1–57505–735–2 (pbk. : alk. paper)
    1. Wit and humor, Juvenile. 2. Nature—Juvenile humor. [1. Nature—Humor.
2. Jokes.] I. Walton, Rick. II. Gable, Brian, 1949– ill. III. Series.
PN6166.S58 2005
818'.60208—dc22   2003019245

Manufactured in the United States of America
1 2 3 4 5 6 – DP – 10 09 08 07 06 05